THE NAME...

JESUS

A Christmas Musical Celebrating
Emmanuel, the King of Kings

Created by Mike Speck
Arranged by Mike Speck and Cliff Duren
Orchestrated by Russell Mauldin, Cliff Duren, and Chris McDonald

Contents

Joy to the World 2

Joy 11

Cherish That Name *with* I Call Him Lord 27

Look Who Just Checked In *with* O Little Town of Bethlehem *and*

　　Angels We Have Heard on High 40

Christ Is Born *with* Angels, from the Realms of Glory *and*

　　O Come, All Ye Faithful *and* Hark! the Herald Angels Sing 54

Glory to God in the Highest (What I Have Been) 65

That Name 75

Worship the Name 91
　　Includes: There's Something About That Name – Jesus, What a Beautiful Name –
　　Emmanuel – Jesus, Name Above All Names

Christ Is Come 103

No Other Name (Underscore) 116

No Other Name 124
　　Includes: No Other Name but Jesus – All Hail the Power of Jesus' Name –
　　O Come, Let Us Adore Him

Drama Notes 136

MS
MIKE SPECK
MUSIC

lillenas
PUBLISHING COMPANY

Joy to the World

Words and Music
Traditional, BURYL RED,
JOSEPH JOUBERT and
MICHAEL MCELROY
*Arr. by Mike Speck
and Cliff Duren*

PLEASE NOTE: Copying of this product is NOT covered by CCLI licenses. For CCLI information call 1-800-234-2446.

CD: 6

Joy

Words and Music by
CHELSEA BENNETT
and ROGER BENNETT
*Arr. by Mike Speck
and Cliff Duren*

(Without music)

WORSHIP LEADER: We have reason to rejoice . . . it's Christmas . . .
and it's the time of year *(Music begins)* that we feast and celebrate.
It's not only the Wise Men rejoicing with exceeding great joy . . . for
good tidings of great joy is for all people throughout all of time. Joy
has come . . . bringing hope, peace and love to all mankind.

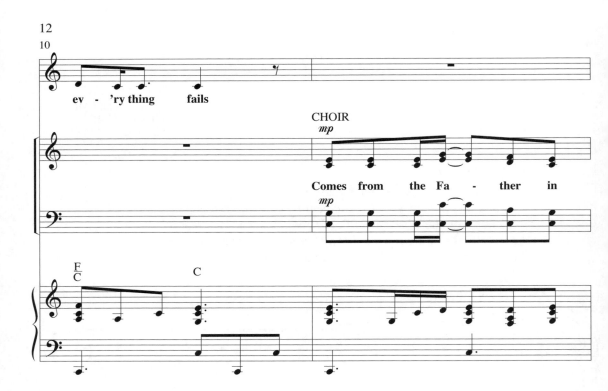

CD: 8

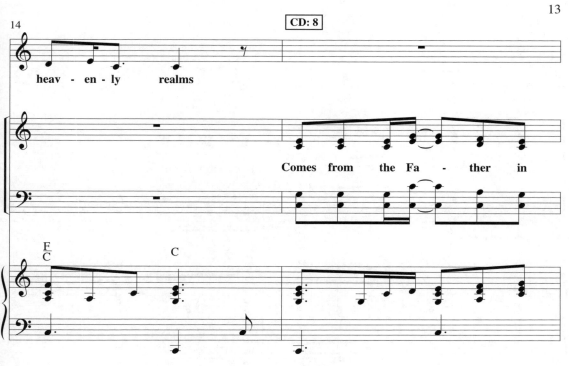

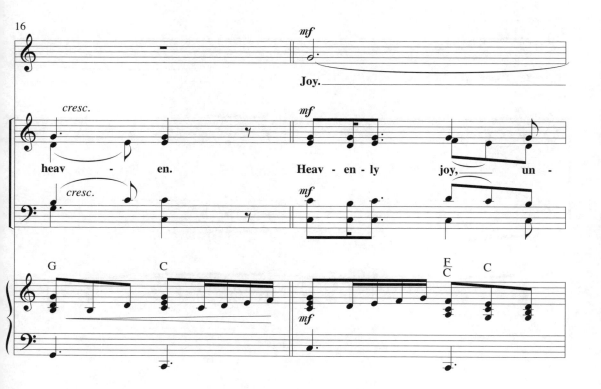

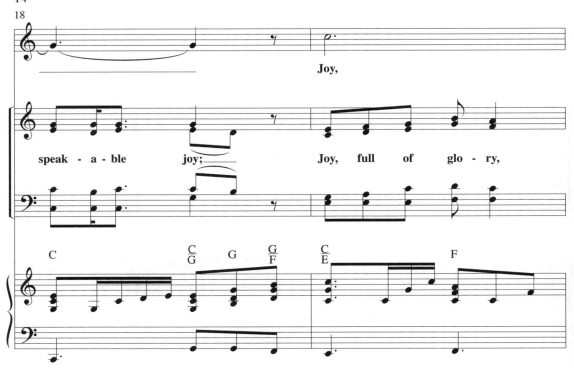

CD: 9

Down from the glo - ries of e - ter - ni - ty,____

Sent from the Fa - ther is heav - en.

O

Je - sus was seek - ing to save you and me,___

A

Gift from the Fa - ther is heav - en.

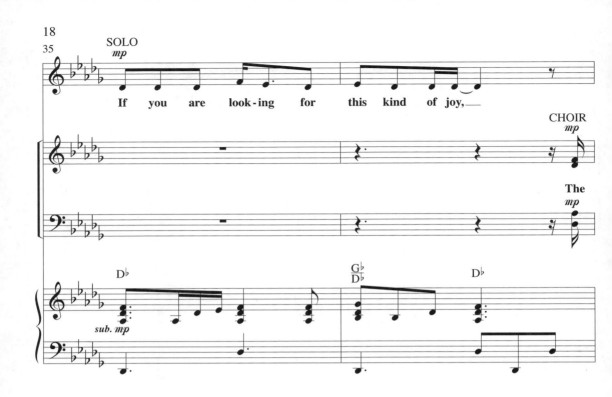

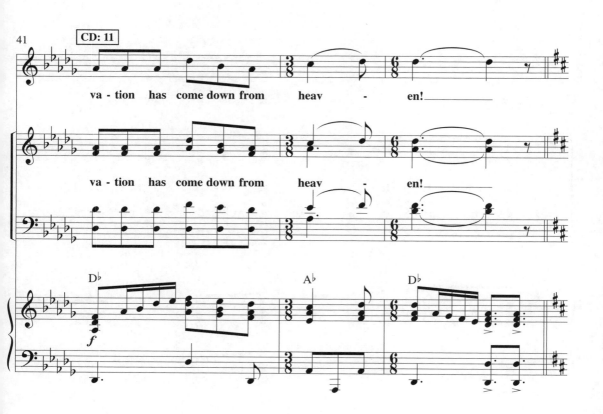

Joy. _____

Won - der - ful joy, _____ mar - vel - ous joy;

Joy, _____ Je - sus is joy.

O what a Sav - ior, Je - sus is joy.

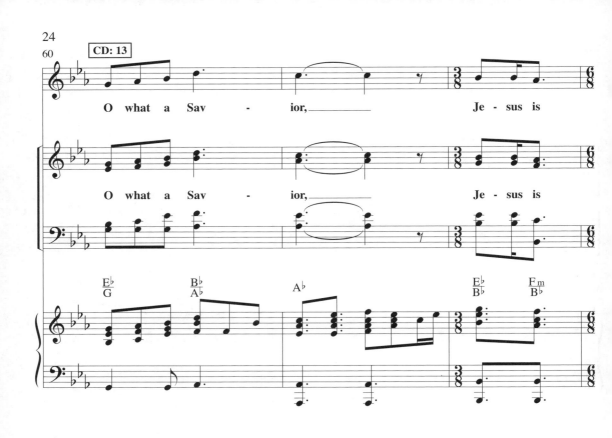

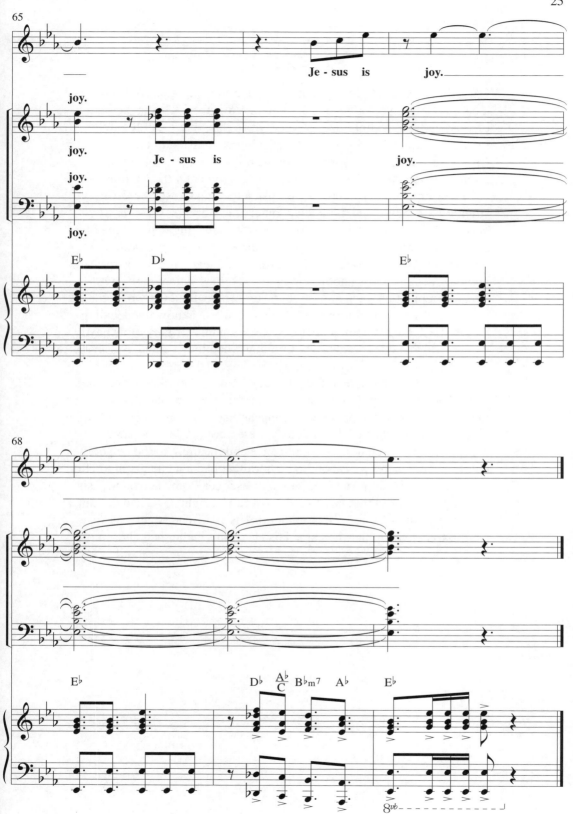

26

(Without music)

WORSHIP LEADER: Joy, rejoicing, laughter and singing have been
a part of Christmas for as long as we can remember. This is the time
of year, and it's the only time of year we do this, that we pull out the
same cassettes, CD's and even record albums, to listen to our favorite
Christmas music. Now some of you won't admit it . . . but you're
going to listen to Manheim Steamroller . . . Alvin and the Chipmunks
. . . The Carpenters . . . some of you listen to Bing Crosby or Elvis
singing blue, blue, blue, blue, blue, blue, blue Christmas, *(in an Elvis
accent)* thank you very much. You know it's amazing that a name like
Elvis could cause such a stir . . . but a name can spark an emotion
(Music begins) or a thought, bring a smile or a tear. You see names are
how we recognize one another. A name becomes synonymous with a
person's reputation, behavior or character. Have you ever wondered
why you were given your name? How many of us know the deciding
factor, the defining moment that gave us our name? Many of us have
wondered what our parents were thinking when they named us. That's
why some of us have nicknames. In the days of the Bible, a name
implied so much more than it does today. A name revealed something
special about the child to which it was given. From an incident during
their birth, to their temperament or appearance . . . from an everyday
object . . . to the time of day that they were born . . . Jewish parents
named their children to give significance and meaning to the newborn
child . . . but a baby was about to be born that had a name given to Him
by God Himself. Jehovah God sent a messenger from Heaven to visit
a young Jewish girl that had found favor in His sight. God had chosen
this pure young lady to be the mother of His son. The angel was very
careful to convey to her the name His Heavenly Father had chosen.

Cherish That Name

with
I Call Him Lord

Words and Music by
LANNY WOLFE
*Arr. by Mike Speck
and Cliff Duren*

Tenderly ♩ = ca. 65

CD: 15 *WORSHIP LEADER: God has chosen . . .*

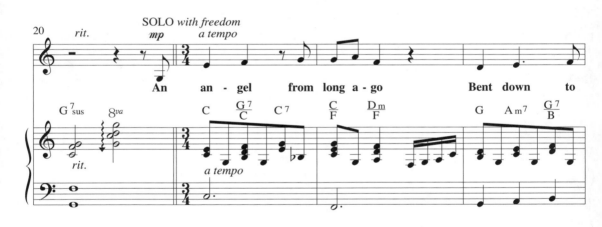

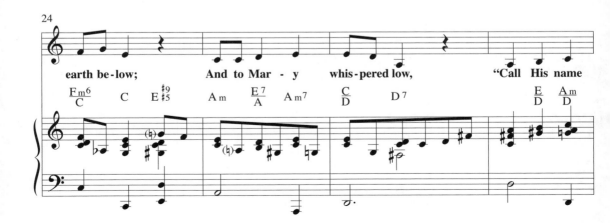

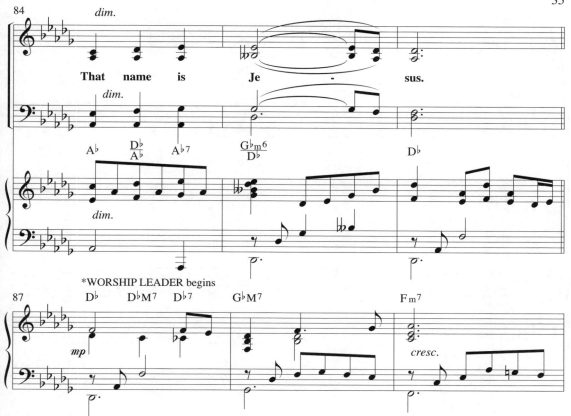

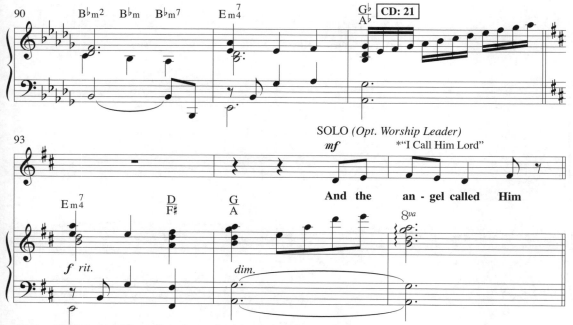

36

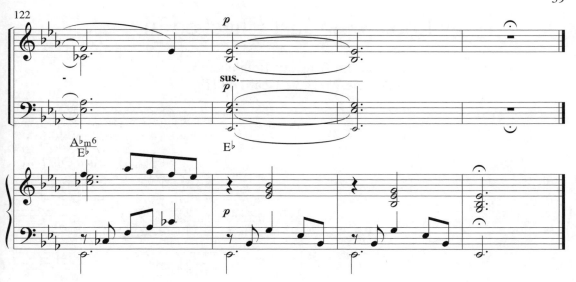

(Without music)

WORSHIP LEADER: There are some distinctive things about Jesus
that cannot be said about any other person . . . beginning with
prophecies that were written concerning His birth. Isaiah spoke
of a virgin girl that would give birth to a son. The prophet, Daniel,
wrote of the precise time in history when the Anointed One would
come. The Psalmist foretold that Kings from the east would visit
Him . . . bearing gifts. Over 700 years before Jesus was born, the
prophet Micah told of the specific location where all of this would
happen. *(Music begins)* He revealed that Bethlehem was the place
where a ruler would be born . . . and that this ruler had origins from
long ago . . . from the days of eternity. So many prophecies and
every one of them, down to the smallest detail were all fulfilled in
this one born in Bethlehem. There had never been nor would there
ever be a baby like Him.

Look Who Just Checked In

with

O Litte Town of Bethlehem
Angels We Have Heard on High

Words and Music by
STEPHEN THOMAS HILL and
DARYL KENNETH WILLIAMS
*Arr. by Mike Speck
and Cliff Duren*

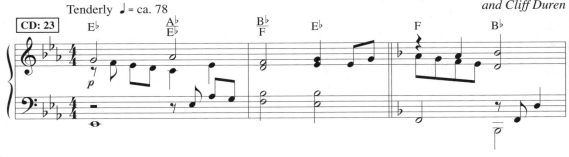

*"O Little Town of Bethlehem"

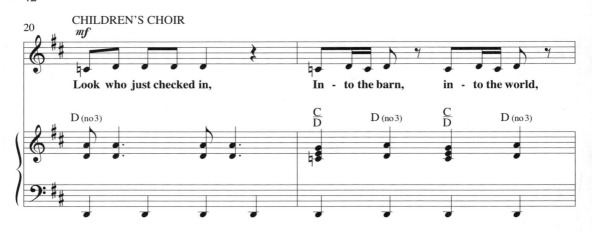

CHILDREN'S CHOIR

Look who just checked in, In - to the barn, in - to the world,

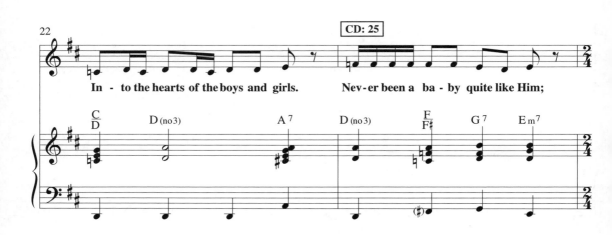

In - to the hearts of the boys and girls. Nev - er been a ba - by quite like Him;

CD: 25

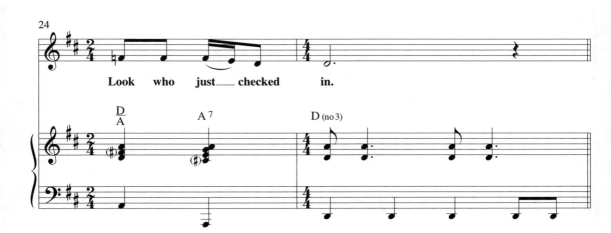

Look who just___ checked in.

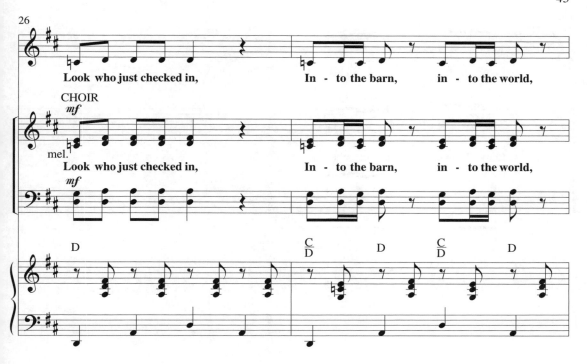

30

Look who just___ checked in.

Look who just___ checked in.

D/A   A7   D(no 3)

*"Angels We Have Heard on High"
ADULT TRIO (or 3-part Choir)

32

mf

Come to Beth - le - hem, and___ see___

D   Bm7   F/A   Em/A   D

34

Him whose birth the an - gels___ sing;___

D   F#♯9/5   Bm7   E7♭9   A7   D   C

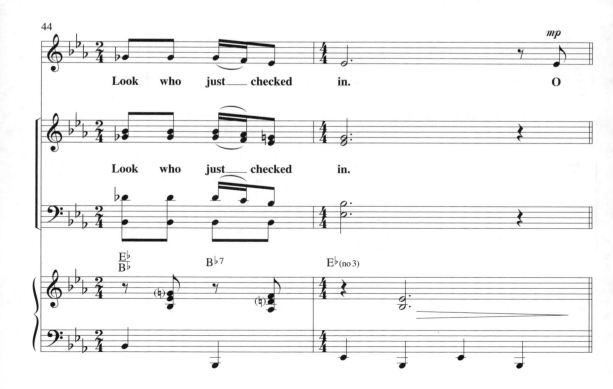

CD: 29

tell it on the moun - tain. Je - sus just checked in!

oo. Je - sus just checked in!

Look who just checked in, In - to the barn, in - to the world,

Look who just checked in, In - to the barn, in - to the world,

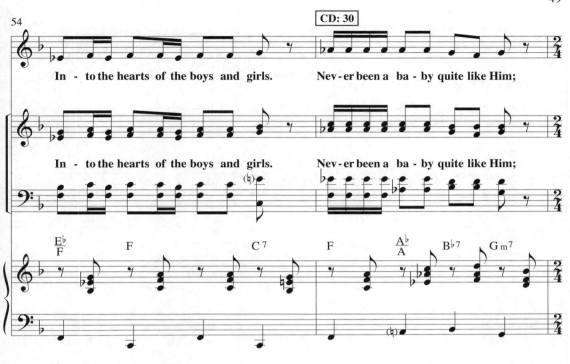

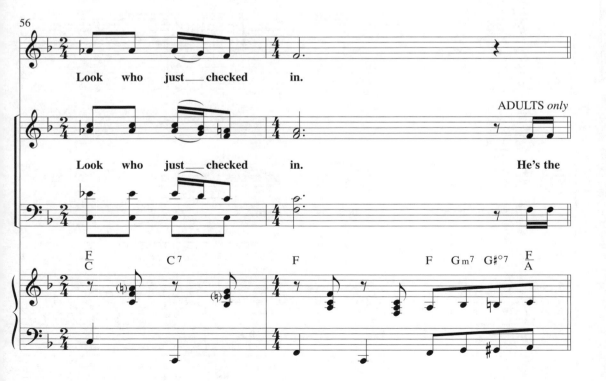

58

Prince of Peace, the King of _ kings; The Lord of the u-ni-verse and ev-'ry liv-ing thing.

B♭   F   C   F

60

Son of God _ since time be - gan. Now He's come to

B♭   F   G⁷

62

CD: 31

Beth - le - hem, Beth - le - hem!

C   D♭

CHILDREN'S CHOIR

f

Look who just checked in, In - to the barn, in - to the world,

Look who just checked in, In - to the barn, in - to the world,

CD: 32

In - to the hearts of the boys and girls. Nev-er been a ba - by quite like Him;

In - to the hearts of the boys and girls. Nev-er been a ba - by quite like Him;

52

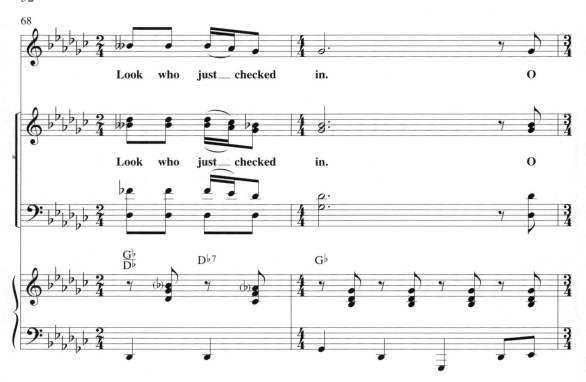

TRIO *and* CHILDREN
(Children sing middle note)

look who just checked in! Check

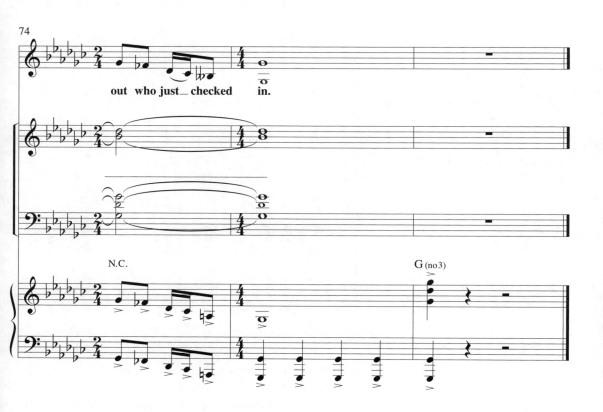

out who just checked in.

Christ Is Born

with

Angels, from the Realms of Glory
O Come, All Ye Faithful
Hark! the Herald Angels Sing

Words and Music by
TIM GREENE
Arr. by Mike Speck
and Cliff Duren

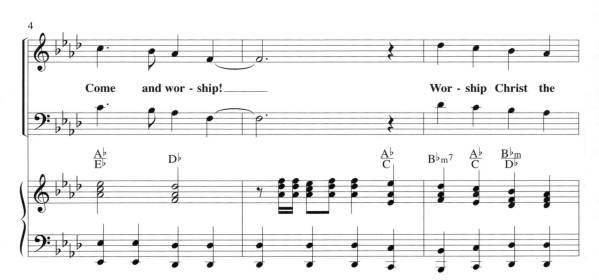

*Words by JAMES MONTGOMERY; Music by HENRY T. SMART. Arr. © 2008 by PsalmSinger Music (BMI). All rights reserved. Administered by The Copyright Company, PO Box 128139, Nashville, TN 37212-8139.

58

*"O Come, All Ye Faithful"

60

CD: 40

Glory to God in the Highest
(What I Have Been)

Words and Music by
RAYMOND MARION SCARBROUGH, JR.
*Arr. by Mike Speck
and Cliff Duren*

*WORSHIP LEADER: The angel proclaimed, "Christ is born," first to a most unsuspecting group of individuals . . . in the darkness of night there was a divine display of sound and lights, startling those who first heard the announcement that a Savior was born. With amazement and wonder, they hurried to the place where the Savior lay.

PLEASE NOTE: Copying of this product is NOT covered by CCLI licenses. For CCLI information call 1-800-234-2446.

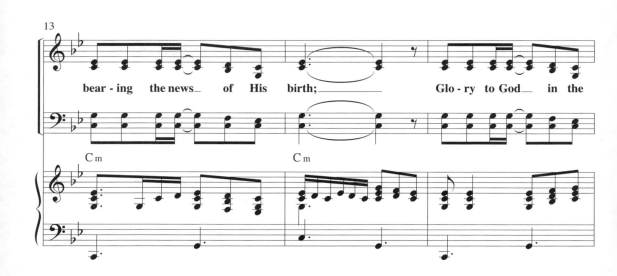

earth._____ Born in the cit - y of

Da - vid,_____ His en - trance so com - mon and

poor;_____ This Ba - by who laid_____ in a

68

74

That Name

Words and Music by
RICHARD SMALLWOOD
Arr. by Mike Speck
and Cliff Duren

(Without Music)

WORSHIP LEADER: What an amazing night for those shepherds on the hills close to Bethlehem. Think about it . . . angels dispatched from Heaven, interacting with ordinary men. Every time I read the Christmas story I see something fresh . . . something new. This year, I noticed the different names attributed to Jesus at His birth. Each name serves as a description of who Jesus really is and how He works in the lives of people. *(Music begins)* The angel, speaking to the shepherds, described the babe in the manger . . . as Savior, He called the One wrapped in swaddling clothes, Christ, which means Messiah . . . the angel also proclaimed that He, Jesus, was Lord. Mary and Joseph were commanded to give the unborn child the name Jesus . . . yet the angel also called Him "Son of the Highest" and "Son of God" . . . and that He would be called "Immanuel," God with us . . . when the Magi came, they inquired, "Where is He who is born King" and where could He be found . . . of all the names, the one that speaks most powerfully . . . is the name Jesus . . . for it is in that name we find the source of all that's good and all that's holy . . . you see, salvation is in that name, healing is in that name, the forces of nature bow to that name, even the demons tremble at the sound of that name. The precious name of Jesus has changed the lives of so many. That name changed me . . . for that name saved me and gave me life . . . and because of that wonderful name . . . I discovered the reason for living . . . I found peace and contentment that the world could never give. I don't know about you, but there is no name more precious or lovely or wonderful than the name Jesus. All that we have ever needed is found in that most matchless name.

CD: 46

prais - es; Be - cause of Him I am made

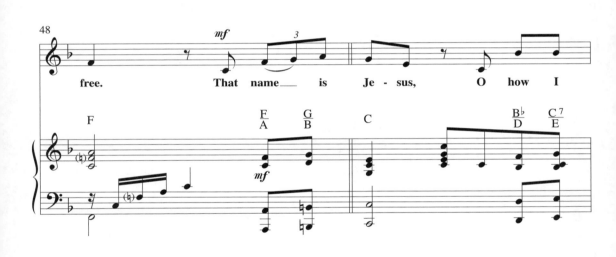

free. That name___ is Je - sus, O how I

love___ Him; The One who gave His life for___

CD: 49

life   e - ter - nal - ly.

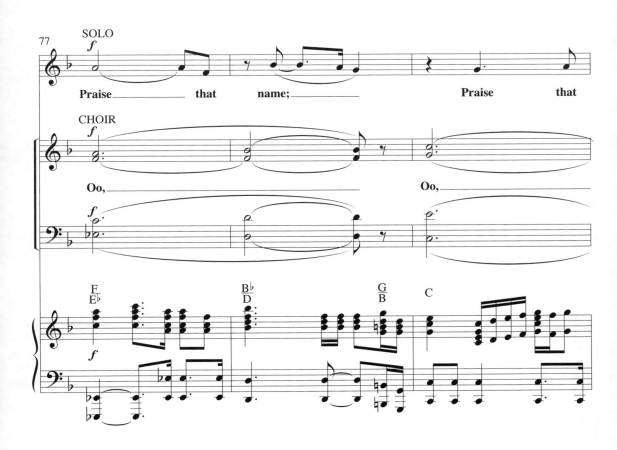

SOLO

Praise_____ that   name;_____   Praise   that

CHOIR

Oo,_____   Oo,_____

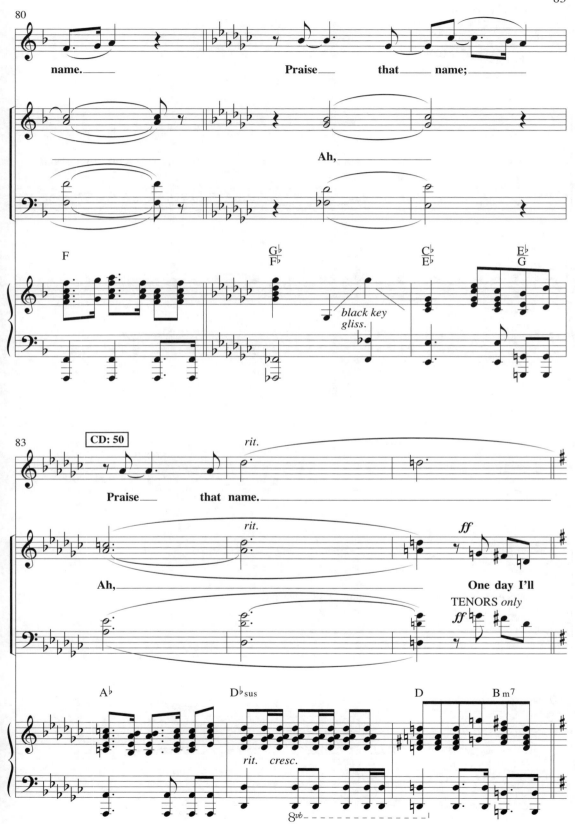

84

88

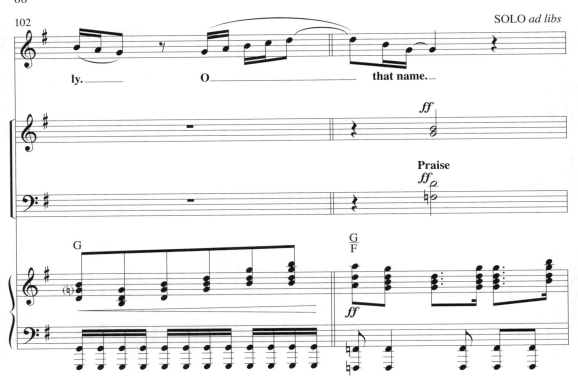

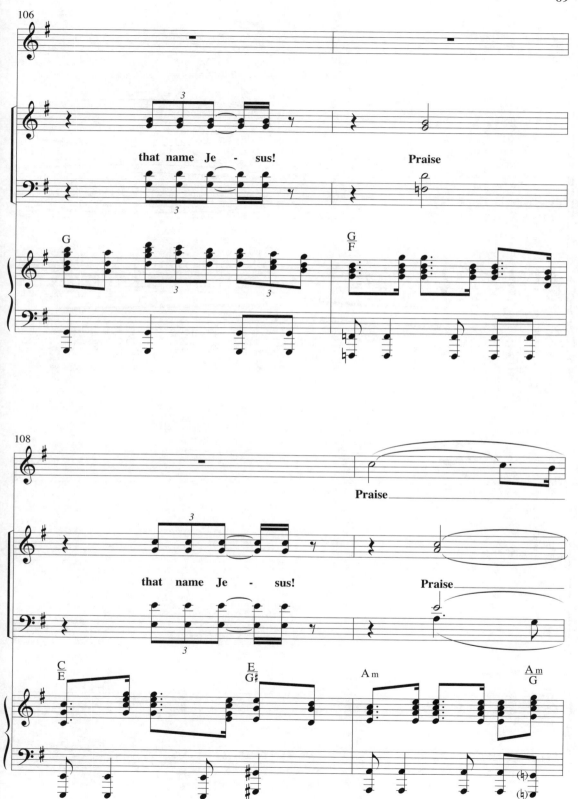

Worship the Name

includes

There's Something About That Name
Jesus, What a Beautiful Name
Emmanuel
Jesus, Name Above All Names

*Arr. by Mike Speck
and Cliff Duren*

(Without music)

WORSHIP LEADER: Sing with me. *(Music begins)*

92

*"Jesus, What a Beautiful Name"
CHOIR

CD: 55

Grace that blows all fear a - way.___ Je - sus,

what a beau - ti - ful name.

Je - sus, what a beau - ti - ful name.

98

CD: 56

85 *"Jesus, Name Above All Names"

Christ Is Come

Words and Music by
MICHAEL DAVID WEAVER
*Arr. by Mike Speck
and Cliff Duren*

*WORSHIP LEADER: We worship that name . . . We give honor and
praise to Jesus, our Redeemer, our Savior, our door to heaven . . .
and we give thanks and praise unto God . . . for sending His own
son . . . Glory to God . . . for Christ, our Messiah is come.

29

Word made flesh now dwells a-mong us;

C m7   B♭/D   A♭2

32

Christ is come!

E♭2   F sus   B♭   B♭/D   E♭2

35   **CD: 61**   LADIES *unis.*
mf

Those born in dark-

B♭   B♭/D   E♭2   B♭/D   E♭2
mf

CD: 62

un - to you   Un - to you,   now un - to you

Christ is come!   Let

all cre - a - tion sing. God's own Son;

110

114

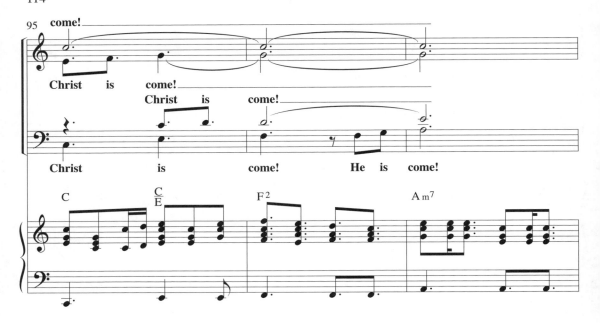

(Without music)

WORSHIP LEADER: Christ is come and we celebrate Christmas because of His arrival. It's an old cliché, but He is the reason for the season. It's hard to fathom that the issue of Christmas, in some circles, has become what to do with Jesus. Banning of manger scenes, renaming Christmas trees, schools removing carols about the birth of Christ . . . what a tragedy . . . for that innocent, perfect baby in Bethlehem is God reaching out to a hurting world, with His love, and His promise of peace, joy and eternal life. Christmas is far more than an annual holiday . . . for Jesus is far more than just a character in a religious story. You cannot constrain Jesus to any particular day . . . for all of History is related to Him. The whole Bible is filled with references to Jesus in one way or another.

(Music begins)

No Other Name

Underscore

Music by
MIKE SPECK and CLIFF DUREN
Arranged by
Mike Speck and Cliff Duren

*WORSHIP LEADER:

(Key of C)

In Genesis: He Is Creator - for all things were made by Him

in Exodus: He's the Deliverer - The Passover Lamb

in Leviticus: He is the Great High Priest - Our Eternal Sacrifice

and in Numbers: Jesus is the Trusted Guide . . . the Cloud in
the daytime and the Pillar of Fire in the darkness of night.

In Deuteronomy: He's the Prophet who is greater than Moses

in Joshua: the Captain of our Salvation . . . the One who leads us
into the Promised Land

in Judges: He is both Judge and Lawgiver

and in Ruth: He is Our Kinsman Redeemer.

(Key of Db)

In Samuel, Kings and Chronicles: He's the Prophet of the Lord and
    the Reigning King

in Ezra: He's the One who fulfills His promises

in Nehemiah: He's the Rebuilder of the Broken and torn down walls
    in our lives

and in Esther: He reveals the providence of God.

(Key of D)

In Job: He is our Ever-Living Redeemer

in Psalms: He is our Shepherd and our Song

in Proverbs: He is Wisdom

in Ecclesiastes: Jesus is our only hope

and in Song of Solomon: He's the Bridegroom, the Rose of
  Sharon, the Lily of the Valley, the Lover of my soul.

(Key of Eb)

In Isaiah: He is Wonderful, Counselor, Mighty God, Everlasting Father,
  the Prince of Peace

in Jeremiah & Lamentations: He's the Potter who puts our broken
  lives back together again.

and in Ezekiel: He's the Watchman of our soul and our High Tower.

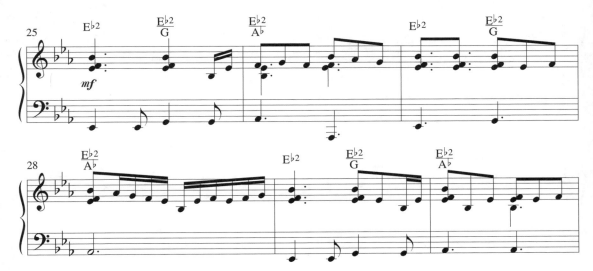

(Key of E)

In Daniel: He's the 4th man in the fiery furnace

in Hosea: He's the Faithful Forgiver and Everlasting Love

in Joel: He is the One who pours out His spirit on all flesh.

in Amos: He is our burden bearer

and in Obadiah: He's our Savior.

120

(Key of F)

In Jonah: He is Merciful and full of grace

in Micah: He is the Ruler called out of Bethlehem

in Nahum: Jesus is our Avenger

in Habakkuk: He is the One who justifies by faith

and in Zephaniah: Jesus is the Lord mighty to save.

(Key of Gb)

In Haggai: He is our Stronghold in a day of trouble

in Zechariah: He is the One whose feet will stand in that day
  on the Mount of Olives as King over all the earth

and in Malachi: He's the Son of Righteousness, rising with
  healing in His wings.

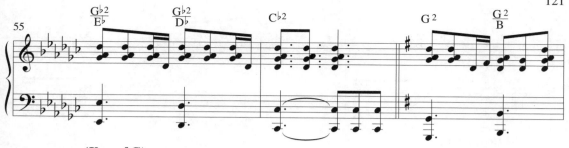

(Key of G)

In Matthew: He's Messiah and King

in Mark: The Wonder-Worker

in Luke: The Son of Man

in John: The Son of God

in Acts: He's our Ascended Lord

in Romans: He is our Salvation

in 1st & 2nd Corinthians: He is Redeemer and the Lord of Glory

and in Galatians: He's the One who sets us free.

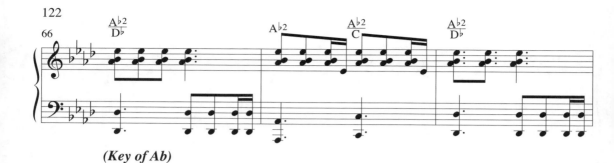

(Key of Ab)

In Ephesians: He's our Chief Cornerstone

in Philippians: He's the God who meets our every need

in Colossians: He's the Hope of Glory

in 1st & 2nd Thessalonians: He's our Soon-Coming King

and in 1st & 2nd Timothy: He's the Mediator between God and man.

(Key of A)

In Titus: He's our Great God and Savior

in Philemon: He's the Friend that sticks closer than a brother

in Hebrews: He's the Blood that washes away my sins

(Key of F)

in James: He's the Great Physician

and in 1st & 2nd Peter: The Chief Shepherd.

In 1st, 2nd & 3rd John: He is our Righteousness, Truth and Love

in Jude: He is the Lord coming with 10,000 saints

and in Revelation: He is the Alpha and Omega, the Beginning
and the End . . . the King of kings and Lord of lords . . .

(Spoken during intro of next song)

Wherefore God has highly exalted him, and given him a name which is
above every name: That at the name of Jesus every knee should bow,
*(of things in heaven, and things in earth, and things under the earth;)
And every tongue confess that Jesus Christ is Lord (to the glory of
God the Father). *(Phil. 2:9-10* KJV *para)*

NOTE: The words in parenthesis can be omitted if time runs out before the vocals enter.

No Other Name

includes
No Other Name but Jesus
All Hail the Power of Jesus' Name
O Come, Let Us Adore Him

*Arr. by Mike Speck
and Cliff Duren*

same. There is no oth - er name.

The first and last, be - gin - ning and the end;

He was the One who made the com - mon man His

126

14

CD: 69

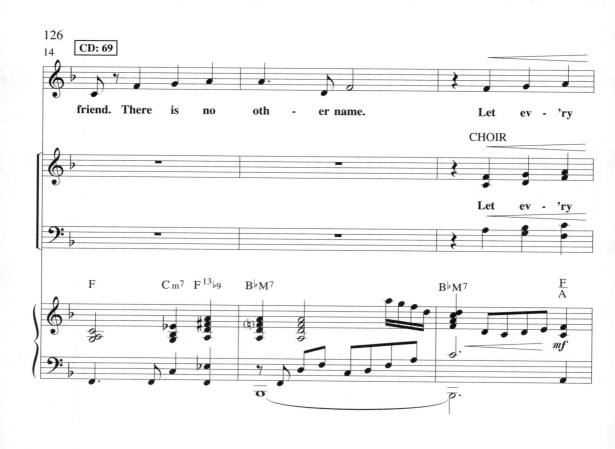

SOLO *ad lib through-out rest of song*

praise the name of Je - sus.

praise the name of Je - sus, Je - sus,

Je - sus, *cresc.*

Je - sus, Je - sus, Je - sus,

CD: 72

*"All Hail the Power of Jesus' Name"

134

*"O Come, Let Us Adore Him"

Broadly ♩ = ca. 62

forth the roy-al di - a - dem, and crown Him Lord____ of____ all. O come, let us a - dore____ Him. Come, let us a - dore____ Him. O

POSSIBLE DRAMA SUGGESTIONS

Cherish That Name

1. There could be a scene where the angel of the Lord is speaking to Mary (at the beginning of the song).
2. It could work for Mary, Joseph and Jesus to appear at a manger with the narration in the middle of the song. (". . . and she brought forth her firstborn son . . .")

Look Who Just Checked In

There could definitely be a manger scene during this festive children's song.

Glory to God

Shepherds have a moment to appear.

Worship the Name

Churches that desire could use this tender moment for their candle lighting.

No Other Name but Jesus

For churches that have a banner ministry, I would suggest bringing them in at "All Hail the Power of Jesus' Name."

Mike Speck